"Full of earnest and joyful contributions that inspire and affirm, this exuberant anthology resonates with love and authenticity. It serves as an earthy and affectionate antidote to a world that suggests that motherhood should be considered an afterthought instead of a priority." — DYMPHNY DRONYK, Q. Med., Senior Consultant & Manager at Communica Public Affairs, President of the League of Canadian Poets Council and Editor/Publisher at blueskiespoetry.ca

"Pope Francis challenges moms and dads to dream about their children… and this little book is a great beginning. I'm a big believer in affirming what is good and in this short work, five spiritually alive mothers make the case brilliantly." — FATHER JULIO LAGOS

"Motherhood shared — whether the ups or the downs — is pure joy, as Melanie Jean Juneau proves again and again in her delightful and insightful writing."
— ALLISON GINGRAS, host of *A Seeking Heart* on Real Life Radio

"There are no cultural boundaries when it comes to love, faith and motherhood. Echoed with laughs and tears, I got inspired by each love rebel's own experiences, honest reflections and ordinary yet spirit-lifting deeds!" — ODILIA LEE, monthly columnist of S.U.C.C.E.S.S. Evergreen News

"*Love Rebel: Reclaiming Motherhood* gives comfort and encouragement to its readers by reaffirming the value of their roles within their families, and as a child of God in their own right."
— LISA WHELTON, Made Just for You By Lisa Designs

"Bonnie Way has a way with words in which you can't help but feel like you are actually there. This book took me back to when my child was small and made me miss all of those things that makes raising a small child so memorable."
— KRISTY-LEA TRITZ, Personal Coach at gettotheheartofthematter.ca

"This beautiful anthology offers wisdom to help us in our calling to bring forth new life — little masterpieces — and bear fruit into eternity. Reclaiming motherhood requires heroic effort!"

— RACHEL LALONDE, artist

"Melanie Jean Juneau's honest reflections on motherhood show the humour as well as the challenge in the daily tasks — and the long-term work — of mothering children."
— BARB SZYSZKIEWICZ, OFS, Editorial Consultant at CatholicMom.com

"Go, rebel moms! Your lives of 'motherhood as a choice and vocation' will sow the seeds of love our culture needs: to encourage us all in a way of love, to challenge our 20th century feminist assumptions and to remind us that a mother's task is a gigantic act of love. These writers give a voice to the challenge and at the same time celebrate it."

— MARY GALLAGHER, Ascend Online homeschooling coach

"What poignant, joyful, valiant and strong witness these 'love rebels' give readers. That most important work of mothers — passing on culture and teaching little ones how to love by loving them — shines through every page of this book." — KATHLEEN HIGGINS, lawyer

"Glad to know the art of mothering has not been lost and I am not the only rebel with a cause. I home-birthed, homeschooled and stayed home to try to make the world a better place like all these mothers."

— DIANNE WOOD, B.Math and Computer Science

"This powerful collection, written by moms worth looking up to, makes me want to be even more rebellious!" — ULRIKA DREVNIOK, RN

Love Rebel

RECLAIMING MOTHERHOOD

An Anthology of 5 Catholic Bloggers

ANNA EASTLAND
MONIQUE LEBLANC
BONNIE WAY
MONIQUE LES
MELANIE JEAN JUNEAU

EDITED BY ROBERTA COTTAM

Love Rebel

Edited by: Roberta Cottam

Contributors:
Anna Eastland
Monique LeBlanc
Bonnie Way
Monique Les
Melanie Jean Juneau

Copyright © 2015

Cover illustration and book design © 2015
by Laura Wrubleski

Print Edition: July 2015
ISBN: 978-0-9940815-3-7

Ebook Edition: July 2015
ISBN: 978-0-9940815-2-0

Published: 2015

Published by: Village Acres Publishing

VILLAGE ACRES
PUBLISHING

In loving memory of
Josephine Pilar Eastland.

* * *

Josephine flashed before us
with the brightness and beauty
of a shooting star

Our hearts are broken by the briefness
of her visit with us

She has climbed onto our Father God's lap
and is whispering to Him our secrets
with sweet confidence
Speak to her in your hearts
the only language she will ever know is love

TABLE OF CONTENTS

FOREWORD

When I became a mom, I struggled to accept descriptions of motherhood as "sacrificing" and "selfless". Yes, there were things I gave up and times my needs came last for the sake of my daughter, but I did not view myself as a "victim" of motherhood.

Few women I knew celebrated their birth stories or breast-feeding experiences, and it was heartbreaking to me that so few mothers spoke joyfully about being vessels for the miracle of life. I believe that being able to bear children is the highest privilege a human can experience, and yet I saw — both personally and in media — a multitude of examples which regarded motherhood as a curse, of sorts. And as such, I met many mothers who were eager to return to work at the end of their maternity leave, myself included.

Though I rebelled at the idea of motherhood being a powerless experience, I struggled all the same with the major transformation that had occurred in my life as a result of bearing a child. I suffered with postpartum depression, and as a result became acutely aware of how our society feeds a new mother's sense of isolation, overwhelm and feelings of inadequacy. I knew there was another way to parent than the perfectionist, competitive and consumerist way my culture had conditioned me to believe.

During the first months following my daughter's birth, my friend Anna Eastland began her blog. Posts on *Just East of Crazy Land* spoke candidly about the triumphs and perils of parenting in a painfully honest and humourous way. This was a voice that spoke a truth I was seeking.

Through Anna, I discovered other bloggers who are up to transforming the landscape of motherhood. These writer-moms offer up a glimpse of their lives, courageously sharing their family philosophies and strategies. Many of these perspectives are directly contrary to mainstream parenting in our culture today: freedom of personal choice throughout pregnancy, midwifery, bearing more children than national averages, home-schooling, backyard homesteading and living a faithful life.

The women featured in this book are rebels in today's birthing and parenting culture. In Anna's article *Modern Motherhood: An Act of Rebellion*, she states that fully devoting one's self to raising children goes against the cultural norms in the western world. I discovered just how right Anna was when I left my job nine months after I'd returned post-maternity leave. As I shared this news with my community, I received feedback that proved my choice was unusual. And though I value my vocation (and will continue to pursue it in a way that better fits my life with children), I knew I was venturing out on a family lifestyle that — in structure — was not the social norm. I became a love rebel.

This book reclaims the vocation of motherhood in all its forms. Melanie Jean Juneau writes about raising nine children in a rural setting; Monique Les about being hard-of-hearing; Bonnie Way about being present to children, no matter the moment; Monique LeBlanc of receiving and learning from our children (and our elders); Anna Eastland about losing a child.

During the compilation of this book, those involved were called to another act of love: to dedicate this project in loving memory of Josephine Pilar Eastland, Anna's sixth child, who passed away on the day of her birth, September 30th, 2014. The week that Josephine died, I conceived my second child. As I mourned Josephine, I welcomed the new soul inside me; this is a tender time that reminds me of how powerful it is for women to share their stories of love incarnate — no matter where the story leads.

To read this book is to celebrate the rebellious acts of love in your life, and to celebrate five noteworthy bloggers from the Catholic community who have embarked on the greatest calling of their lives: motherhood.

Roberta Cottam
July 2015

SLEEP DANCE

Roberta Cottam

Baby soft palms slap my shoulder blades
pat my rib cage, eyelashes flutter
across my collarbone and her head is heavy on my throat
one hand explores my face
pinches my nose squeezes my lips pulls on the flesh of my cheek

She sneezes
then me
I yawn
then she
a foot in my belly
a second on my knee, toes clench unclench

This dance is called sleep, to her
but for me, a vivid night out of my life
when my partner will never dance this way again

Anna Eastland

Montse (age 7): Mummy, it's a good thing you got married and had kids, 'cause your job is blogs, and otherwise you wouldn't have much to write about.

BELLY POEM

There's a poem in my belly
encrypted in code
a little tiny story
waiting to be told

It's curled up tight
in its tiny red room
little tiny heart beating
to the rhythm of my womb

On publishing day
it will be so fine
to see my little poem
come out and shine

Its path in the world
is yet unknown
but with time and love
it will be shown

Then my little poem
will shout out its song
unfurl its beauty
and sweep us along

Its story is just starting
but it'll end never
'cause this little belly one
is a poem to last forever

MODERN MOTHERHOOD: AN ACT OF REBELLION

For a society seemingly obsessed with personal freedom, our culture likes to impose a lot of claims about what we can't do. We are told many things are impossible, dangerous or — Heaven forbid — antiquated. Motherhood is one of these things.

Some of my friends have told me their own mothers have expressed disappointment at their daughters choosing motherhood as a full-time profession. Their mothers have said things like:

"What a waste of your education!"

"Are you living in the Middle Ages?"

"Who is forcing you to have all these kids?"

"What about your career?"

"I don't want you to end up like I did."

For me, this is very sad, because it shows me how deeply the women of our mothers' generation have been convinced that their lives were a waste. It almost implies that after all the work of feminism to open up career options for women, it's dysfunctional for us to want a family. That we are not living up to our mothers' expectations of us as modern women if we choose to follow in their footsteps.

We could ask our moms, "Do you regret spending your life

with me so much? I would not be here without you. Was I really a mistake?"

There is something very messed up here. It doesn't feel right to deny the value of love...I can't understand a feminism that says that something as essentially feminine as motherhood is a waste of time. I'm all for women having freedom and career options, but can feeling that we must imitate our fathers and reject our mothers be pro-woman?

We are told our lives as women will be over if we become moms, but according to whose definition of life? A baby brings new life, adventure, hope, and community. Many of my best friends are fellow moms who are like sisters to me. I feel so lucky that we can spend time together while doing the important work of raising our children and caring for our homes. Laughing and crying with them has helped me get through many long days.

We women get to form deep friendships. How many men regularly have the time to spend with close friends, exploring life and encouraging each other? Many are instead very lonely, and yet if we moms are open to it, there is a vast array of women waiting to be our friends.

Perhaps the money mantra comes to mind...that staying home with the kids is a luxury for the rich. But that's not true either. My husband and I got married out of university, and had nothing but our love and a huge student loan debt. I was on maternity leave the first year and have been home with the kids (5 and counting) ever since. We've done it on one income, while paying off our huge loans (now gone, thank goodness).

Certainly we had to make some sacrifices. We lived in a

one-bedroom apartment with our two little girls and baby. Our living room had a set of bunk beds and a bassinet in it. Now we have a large two bedroom with double bunk beds. We still don't have a car, and use public transit.

But you know what? It's fine! The kids are happy being together; they crave closeness and give each other so much attention and love. "When can the baby sleep in our room?" they asked me when our fourth was born. Sure a little more space would be nice, but which one of my children would be worth giving up for an extra bedroom, a vacation or a vehicle? Can you imagine trading in your toddler for a new Honda Civic?

We've actually hardly had to buy a thing except food and diapers. People are very generous when you are open to it, and my kids don't have to be that expensive. They are happy with simple things, like playing with a sibling in a box, or emptying the Tupperware cupboard; why spoil this by loading them with unnecessary material possessions? The real challenge is stopping doting relatives from doing so!

It's true my days are busy. I don't suffer from boredom. But seemingly busier than ever, I've finally found time for art. It wasn't until I had five kids that I finally started writing regularly. My blog is called *Just East of Crazy Land* for a reason, but as long as I take a few minutes to step back, breathe and pray, my busy days with the kids are full of inspiration and laughter. Often I have to drop my housework to jot down ideas on my iPad. I'm physically engaged, but my mind is free enough to run on a deeper track, to see beauty in the chaos and find meaning in the challenging work I do.

Sure, kids are a lot of work, but what worthwhile endeavour

isn't? Is creating a home not worthwhile just because you don't get paid? Remember that money isn't everything and doesn't actually determine our real worth. As human beings, we can imbue every kind of decent work with love and meaning, even dishes and diapers. British author Gilbert Keith Chesterton put it well in his book *What's Wrong with the World:*

"When domesticity is called drudgery, all the difficulty arises from a double meaning in the word. If drudgery only means dreadfully hard work, I admit the woman drudges... But if it means that the hard work is more heavy because it is trifling, colourless and of small import to the soul, then...I give it up; I do not know what the words mean."

To focus exclusively on physical challenges and chores is to have a ludicrous view of raising children, equivalent to that of herding sheep or feeding pigs. Children are not mere bodies to be cared for, they are human beings to be raised. They are emerging intellects and budding souls; they are creative spirits fascinated by the world. They want to know everything and look to their mothers to explain it:

"Look, Mummy, if I plant this feather will it become a flower?"

"Can I snuggle the new baby in your tummy while we watch a movie, and then you can put her back?"

"Why is the bad guy mean?"

Chesterton asks us:

"How can it be a large career to tell other people's children about the Rule of Three, and a small career to tell one's own children about the universe? No; a woman's function is laborious, but because it is gigantic, not because it is minute."

So I encourage my fellow mothers to be rebels of love. Rebel against a culture which says that motherhood doesn't matter… that raising children is a trivial mindless job, unfit for modern women. Rebel against the idea that serving yourself is the only way to happiness. Rebel against a culture which says that the gift of life is not worth giving.

Do you have to choose a power suit and a government-taxed salary over a lasting marriage and a beautiful family? You can work and be involved in society and contribute to making the world a better place as a woman, but among many other ways it can be through the challenging, amazing, and fulfilling vocation of educating the future citizens of the world, your children.

REMEMBER

I remember sprawling in the grass
in my shorts and t-shirt
making a perfect imprint of myself in the ground
seven years old and utterly at home
as the afternoon sun pulsed red
through my closed eyes

Nothing but the singing of birds
and whisper of butterfly wings in my ears
no thoughts
nothing beyond the moment
perfectly content

Now I'm thirty-two years old
and nine months pregnant
leaning back in my lawn chair
as my toddler snuggles in my lap
and gives me Eskimo kisses

Our resident hummingbird sings heartily
unphased by the vroom and bang
of townhouse construction next door

The faint familiar scent of cut plywood
wafts over the fence to blend with the smell of garden manure

My five-year-old feeds the chickens
one scrap at a time
and gives me a play by play:
"Rosie ate a piece of lettuce off Chickeny's back
and the brown chickens are fighting over a tomato."
"Mmmm...so funny," I reply sleepily

That same afternoon sun pulses down
red on my closed eyelids
and out of my mind
too tired for thoughts
begins to float poetry

MIDWIVES SUPPORT THE BEAUTIFUL MYSTERY OF MOTHERHOOD

For all of my six children, including the one due this fall, I've been cared for by midwives. My experience of pregnancy and birthing has been one of support, encouragement, friendship and admiration. My midwives have made it clear that they are simply here to support me in this amazing work of my body. Their faith in a woman's ability to bring forth new life, to do this miraculous thing called giving birth, has been very affirming of the beauty and strength of being a woman.

Experiencing a number of births has given me the chance to learn some things, with the assistance of my midwives. I've learned that being physically active during pregnancy helps labour go more smoothly. We don't have a car so I walk a lot, and chasing around my other little ones keeps me busy, too. I always joke that they are my portable gym; I don't have to pay anything to keep fit!

I've learned that it's best to not be too attached to a birthing plan, because a huge part of birth is letting go, and the stress of hanging on to fixed ideas makes it harder. Relax and surrender. None of the process will matter that much once you look into your baby's eyes for the first time and realize this little miracle is yours to love forever.

I've learned that birthing in the water is amazingly

supportive of the body during the intense work of labour; it gives relief from the pressure of gravity and warmth to embrace you while you are in pain. It's also easier to shift position and pace yourself when the strong urge to push comes on...helping you prevent tearing by letting baby come out too fast. Most of my babies were born in the water, where it's warm, wet and familiar; they hardly cried and were able to nurse easily after a little skin-to-skin snuggle time.

I've learned that labour is hard work, and makes you hungry, and when cold hospital sandwiches don't cut it after giving birth, the best thing your husband can do is order pizza for you! Warm, sweetened tea with milk helps restore blood sugar as well, and gets your body back on track after eating so little while in labour. Lemonade helps to sustain you while you're still at it!

I've learned that you have to be gentle with yourself after birth, and that the more you rest at first, the better you'll recover in the long run. There is a lovely tea by Celestial Seasonings called Tension Tamer which helps with the after-cramps as your uterus shrinks back to its normal golf or tennis ball size. Of all things it's the catnip in it which helps with cramps...who knew!

I've learned that nursing can make you even hungrier than pregnancy, so have lots of good snacks like granola bars, trail mix, yogurt, muffins and easy meals on hand (spanakopita is my favourite with a newborn). Also, never refuse someone who wants to help out somehow. Let your friends organize a meal train for you and receive them joyfully in your pyjamas. Don't try to pretend you've miraculously recovered after a week or two. It takes time. Be humble and let someone else be the hero for you.

All this helps build community and fosters an environment of support and love in which to raise your children. As my midwives wisely told me, remember that in caring for yourself during pregnancy and after, you are modelling how to do so for your daughters. Treat yourself as you want them to treat themselves one day. And don't be afraid to ask for their help either. Children can be heroically sweet and helpful when they understand how much they can help mummy and the new baby. They are proud to be useful members of your family, in ways big or small.

My midwives have a sense of awe and beauty around one of the most sacred things we human beings can do: incarnate our love and share it with the world. They treat carrying a child as an act of strength and love rather than a mere medical condition or a problem to be solved with lots of intervention. The challenges of pregnancy have been supported and worked though together, as part of the reality of being fully woman… a person not to be pitied but to be praised.

Motherhood is a beautiful thing, perhaps even more so because it requires some sacrifice. Perhaps we don't like that word, but nor do we like selfishness. We admire heroes because they care about something bigger than themselves. Choosing to love even when it hurts is a sign of strength.

Family is a blessing, and being a woman is a great privilege. May we never forget it, or cease to be grateful for being able to participate in the mystery and miracle of bringing new life into the world. I can honestly say that I'm more in awe every time I give birth…and holding your newborn for the first time never gets old!

EVENING ROMANCE

Tonight I feel wrapped in romance
listening to mellow piano solos
and dancing with you

All the highschool dances
I danced alone
cease to matter

Every girlish dream
for a love worth serenading to the stars
fulfilled

Imaginings of dancing ballet
on a grand stage with sparkling lights
played out here in my living room
under the glowing Christmas lights
I still have up
though it's past New Year's

Not needing a million romances
I've found one love
to make my heart overflow

my sweet husband, my best friend
our four little girls
with all their hugs and laughter
and you, my adorable baby son
sleepy little lovely you

THE PERFECT PARENT LIVES IN TIMBUKTU (AND IS LIKELY A SASQUATCH)

I haven't met the perfect parent. It's not me. It's likely not you either.

But that's okay. Children are born of love, not perfection.

Still, sometimes we wonder if there is a scientific formula for being the perfect parent, a special combination of elements that will help us get it just right.

Our society encourages this; we are told we must have the right economic, educational, medical, emotional, and intellectual circumstances to responsibly have a child. It seems a very dangerous and risky business, and one must be perfectly prepared.

Sometimes people wait their whole lives to be ready. Baby room painted just so. Millions in the bank. Eight hundred parenting books read. Relationship so stable it makes mountains look wispy and wobbly. Health just so, taking the right sixty vitamins, and doing yoga ten hours a day.

What happened to something that used to be so natural? A creative overflow of love? Isn't the sincere love between parents already giving your child a lot, especially in today's world?

But our fear of being imperfect parents in an imperfect world paralyzes us so much as a society. We fear traumatizing our kids and are haunted of visions of their future therapist's couch before they even leave their cradle.

We are told we better consult the experts constantly, because we as "mere parents" (just rabbits really) know nothing. I don't think all this fear is actually making us better parents, just less confident and optimistic ones.

If we risk having one child, we think we shouldn't have another, because we're not perfect yet. The funny thing is though, that having another child helps us to grow better — more mature, relaxed and confident — and therefore helps our first child, too. Experience is a good teacher.

So please don't let fear of your imperfection stop you from loving; that would be a terrible tragedy. None of us had perfect parents, but we're still glad to be here, in this messy, imperfect, absurdly beautiful world.

While I haven't met perfect parents, I have met perfect babies.

Actually many of them.

More specifically, all of them.

Each baby is perfect.

A perfect gift, a perfect miracle, a perfect parcel of love.

Each one makes the world more beautiful. That means you, too.

Siblings help each other to grow as well, precisely through their imperfection, their foibles and stubborn streaks… experiencing all this helps children learn, in a context of love, how to get along with, embrace and accept others.

If we are teaching our kids to love, to care for others and help them when they are down, we are doing a lot toward making the world a better place.

My kids can squabble as much as the next ones, but I was

happy to see my older girls stepping up and caring for the younger ones this week when they weren't feeling well. For example, my five-year-old read bedtime stories to her little sister. Without being asked. That made me really happy.

So stop worrying about being perfect, unless you want to go live with the Sasquatch, who can maybe give you some pointers.

Personally, I think what you need as a parent is love, commitment and a willingness to adapt and grow, because as much as parenting will make your children grow, it'll make you grow more. Children are gifts, and with them comes the grace and help to care for them. Think of each child as a vote of confidence from your Creator who chose you to help Him make the world more beautiful.

Happy trails! And may you be abundantly blessed in love.

ONLY STILLNESS

!!
All of a sudden
the lights are out
at 7 pm
just as we're starting dinner

It becomes a candlelit meal
peaceful
our family enclosed
in a small circle of light
my children's faces
illuminated by the tiny flames

There is nothing else to rush to
no dishwashers or dryers
no email or phone
so we linger around the table laughing
as our three-year-old
makes up silly stories about babies
and bunnies and when she was little
and used to be a toy and a chocolate

The kids pile easily into their new double bunk beds
with the LED lantern lighting up
their imaginary campground

The baby gives up
cooing at the candle
and lets me rock him to sleep

It is so quiet
there is only stillness
and this small circle of light

THE MYSTERY OF LOSING A LITTLE ONE

So many mothers and fathers suffer the loss of a baby through miscarriage in relative silence, and are left to heal alone. I have always thought we should support them more, and encourage them to share their stories. Little did I know that after five healthy births we would suddenly lose our sixth child during labour. Now I have a story of my own.

We lost baby Josephine on September 30th this year, a day before the start of Pregnancy and Infant Loss Awareness Month. It seems the cord was tightly wrapped around her neck, and she faded into Heaven in early labour. When she was born looking like a beautiful sleeping newborn, it was hard to believe. We held her almost all night. I wanted so desperately to make her warm. Leaving the hospital the next night without my baby was one of the hardest things I've ever done.

And yet I realize we are incredibly blessed. Most people who lose children through early miscarriage don't get the chance to cuddle and kiss them. Theirs is a more hidden loss. But I want to affirm that they also truly lost a loved one. They had their hopes dashed and their world shaken. They need prayers, support, and the presence of family and friends just like anyone who has lost a child at any stage, no matter how recently or long ago. They need to be able to talk about their loss without worrying that they might make people uncomfortable.

Sometimes they'll need to laugh with you, other times to cry. I can tell you that what a grieving parent needs is not for you to try to make it all better by saying the right thing; it is simply to listen sympathetically, and to assure them of your love and prayers. It is to walk with them on this journey towards healing, realizing that life for them won't simply go back to normal. It may be deeper, richer, and more meaningful, but it will never be the same.

Praying in a little chapel two weeks after I delivered Josephine, I asked, "God, why did you break my heart in two?"

He answered, "To make it bigger."

"Okay. That's a good reason." Then I implored our Lady, "Mama, will you teach her all about Jesus? I never got the chance."

"Oh, there's no need." She smiled. "She knows Him already."

"Okay. That works, too."

The mysteries of suffering and grace are intertwined in solemn beauty when you lose a little one. When your heart breaks, you discover something very important, that while it is incredibly painful, you've never been closer to Heaven. "The kingdom of God is within" changes from being a familiar phrase into a tangible reality, because your baby, whom you are sure is in God's embrace, is at the same time inextricably connected to you. It's as if a window has been ripped into Heaven, and you can peek in.

Grief has a way of breaking down walls. It shatters superficial barriers and exposes our vulnerability. It can unite us, despite any other differences, because we all can suffer, and we all can love. Sharing grief is an opportunity for healing and growth, and creates an intimate bond that gives us strength. We are not alone. This is good to remember when we lose someone we love, no matter how small.

When we suffer deeply but without losing our hope, we become powerful witnesses to the joy of being children of God. We affirm the sacredness of the gift of life, and the goodness of a life lived trusting in Providence. We don't need to know the answer to every "why?" because we know that God loves us immensely and has a plan for us, even when we don't understand it. The why doesn't matter in the end, because it won't bring our child back. Life is a mystery lived in love.

When a little one dies, our illusion of control disappears. But God gives us something greater, the tangible feeling of His hands carrying us through the darkness, and the knowledge that each moment of life is a gift.

There is a scripture quote from Jeremiah that helped me to feel that Josephine's brief life on earth had purpose and meaning:

"Before I formed thee in the womb I knew thee; and before thou camest forth out of the womb I sanctified thee, and I ordained thee a prophet unto the nations." Jeremiah 1:5

I want to end by assuring all parents who have lost children at any age that their little ones have a great mission: to inspire others to love. Our babies do this by their simple fact of existing; they are a witness to God's beauty and goodness, and their innocent lives inspire others to generosity and kindness. May your little saints in Heaven ever guide you and bring you hope.

DULL ACHE

Dull ache
like I've fallen flat on face
Grey skies
match my insides
It's hard to talk
about her today
The pain throbs
in a delicate way
that won't leave
I'm sitting here
eating Cheerios without cheer
My little ones laugh
and sing
but I don't feel like doing a thing
Strange day
now that she's gone away
The neighbourhood seems
empty and odd
Life's going on
people bustling away
But I'm in this bubble
floating above
feeling lost
without my little love

CLOSER THAN EVER

The grass is still green
on this side of the world
The sun still shines red
through my eyelids
It warms my upturned face
as the fall leaves fall
with delicate grace
Children still laugh
and the birds still fly
Flowers open and close
You're gone away
little one
but closer than ever
No longer does your heart
beat in my body
That quick little drum
has faded now
But now that you've gone
to be with the stars
you've ripped open my heart
exposed Heaven within and
I've found you
closer than ever
here in my soul

Anna Eastland

Vancouver, British Columbia

eastofcrazyland.wordpress.com
anna-eastland.barefootbooks.com

Born with midwives in her grandmother's house in Wild Rose Country, Alberta, Anna has lived all over British Columbia, and spent part of her teenage years in Holland. Named Anna Rose after a girl in a storybook, Anna has loved writing since she was tiny and holds a BA in English and Classical Studies from UBC. She's a blogger, Barefoot Books sales representative, professional homemaker and homeschooling mom of five with one more in Heaven. She and her husband James recently celebrated nine years of marriage.

Monique LeBlanc

Me to my 12-year-old: Hey, what do you think of my outfit?
12-year-old: It looks like you are trying to look sexy and modest at the same time.
Me: I sort of am.
12-year-old: Well, it doesn't work.

WHY I DO WHAT I DO

So many days I think, "Why do I do the things I do?"

Why do I get up to make lunches that I know no one will eat? Why wash dishes that are only going to get dirty again (and clothes and floors, and windows and toilets — ahh, the list keeps going)? Why do I keep reminding, explaining (nagging) to be polite, respectful and kind? Why, oh why do I keep breaking up fights, drying tears and helping to mend broken relationships (and toys)?

And then there are those rare days when the sun breaks through the clouds for a few moments and I can see. Like when my eldest son gets up to wash dishes without being asked. Or I see him serving the altar so big and confident. When my kids say, "You know, you are a good mom," and not because I gave them candy.

When that shy clingy child, who I was told would never learn to let me go if I did not force her to be without me, is running to meet new friends, getting on stage to play her fiddle or excelling at school.

And there are other days when things are bad. I find out that one of my kids is being bullied. But I have the time to sit and let them cry until they can tell me what is happening. Time to go to the school and talk to the principal and teachers and be part of the healing.

There was that week at family music camp where every day someone different came up to me to say how wonderful my kids are, how polite and respectful. What wonderful parents we are. (I still wonder if they could see my kids running around the house at top speed and volume if they would say the same thing.)

You know, I am really proud of what I do. I used to be embarrassed when I would have to answer the question, "What do you do for a living?" Like the answer, "I'm home with the kids," was somehow lazy or boring.

But now I say it with pride. What I do every day is often boring, menial work. Sometimes what I do is exhausting. Sometimes I want nothing more than to put on a nice outfit and sit in an office where they give you coffee breaks and let you go to the bathroom all by yourself. But what I do is the most important work I could ever do. And I am starting to see the fruit of what I have been doing for twelve years now. I can see that the time spent reading, playing, holding and loving are paying off. Not for me, but for them. It is just beginning but I can see them growing into these amazing people, exploring and learning beyond me. And you know, I love it. I love seeing the glimpse of who they will be. I (sort of) love being left behind with only a wave goodbye.

They won't remember every bandaid, every storybook, every reminder to say thank you. And I don't want them to. I want them to be thinking about the horizon, the next adventure, their life. And I hope I get a few phone calls and visits. And a little time to see more of the results of my work.

SACRED IN THE MUNDANE

A friend of mine emailed me the other day to let me know that she was expecting another baby. This is of course exciting even if not overly surprising. This is their sixth child and every one of them have been a welcomed blessing. In fact, babies in their family and the world are a normal every day occurrence. I have lots of friends who are expecting a baby or have just had one. Babies are born every day, lots of them. You would think that such a normal thing would not bring us surprising joy, yet everyone calls babies "miraculous" and they are.

Is it any surprise then that God brought the biggest miracle of all to us in the same "ordinary" way. What is so special about a young mother having a baby? What is so wonderful about the news "unto us a child is born"? Isn't that every day news? Why would God not do something more amazing? I don't know — like a big, fiery, explosive entrance.

But you know, that is not how I have seen God working in the world. Usually He comes in the every day ways. In the smile of a friend, the beautiful sunset, that still quiet feeling that comes when you know that you are on the right track.

I am not denying that God can and does do big miracles. And hey, a big choir of angels in the sky is a pretty big thing, but for most of us, most of the time God comes in the every day.

Today I saw Him in the laughter of my kids. I felt His presence as I kneaded bread dough. The trick is to see Him, recognize Him in those moments. Most of the time I miss Him. But that is okay, He will be there again. In the next ordinary moment.

STRENGTH THROUGH THE GENERATIONS

This spring and summer we were blessed to host Ryan's grandparents several times. As octogenarians, they still live in their own home in a small town about two hours away. On occasion they need to come into the city for various appointments. In some ways this can be stressful. For one thing I need to keep the house clean. This is not easy for a mother of five.

Having them stay also means that my attention is focused on them instead of on the kids. But these small hardships can never outweigh the vast blessing of having them. This was made clear to me in two beautiful ways recently.

Grandpa has been cleaning out his office and found a collection of pennies dating back to the 1910s. Unsure what to do with it, he brought it to us thinking if we did not want to keep it at least we could sell them. Our oldest was enthralled. So, for hours Grandpa and great-grandson sat with piles of coins and a magnifying glass. They talked and listened, shared stories and organized the coins. My son now has a coin collection but more than that he has a deepening relationship with a man that has lived through the depression, WW2, who started teaching in a one room school house and who has stayed active and generous through a retirement that has lasted longer than his teaching career.

During another visit, Great-grandma and Great-grandpa and our littlest sat finishing lunch. I was cleaning up, and putting away the leftovers. Just like every three-year-old, she wanted to help so I gave her a small piece of crumpled plastic to wrap up her half eaten cookie. She sat patiently straightening out the plastic wrap while Grandpa looked on. I thought nothing of it but later that week Grandma told me over the phone that Grandpa was inspired. Apparently, before their visit, every time the plastic wrap got stuck together Grandpa gave up, threw it out and got a new piece. But now, he says, "If your great-granddaughter can do it, then so can I."

I have often thought how much we have to learn from these amazing people: how to grow a garden to feed you for the whole winter; how to knit, sew and make cool things out of wood; how to be married for sixty-two years; how to stay strong and committed through the loss of children, professional insecurity and failing health.

But I am learning that we have a lot to give to them too — the energy of youth, the simple joy of a child's smile. On their last visit, Grandma said that we are a force of healing for her. And I see it. I see how sitting and reading to the kids, seeing them run around with laughter and sharing their stories to eager ears gives life to these venerable people.

WHY MY KIDS DO CHORES

I am a strong believer in chores. Yes, there is a selfish component in that. I hate cleaning and I can use all the help I can get.

But really, that's not it. For the most part, having the kids do chores is more work for me, not less. For one thing, I have to get them to *do* them. I also have to get all the stuff out for them, help them along the way and "inspect" to make sure it is done. Plus, I have to put up with it done their way and not mine.

So if a clean house with no effort from me is my goal I am way better off hiring a cleaning team and depriving my children of all luxuries and some basic needs to pay for it. There would be less whining.

The real reason I have my kids to chores is that it is good for them.

First off, it teaches them that we are a team. This is *our* house, not my house with them as guests. We all live here and we all have to take care of it together. I hope that this lesson will carry over to the idea that we are also a team in other ways. We all have to take care of each other. We are family for life and if your brother or sister needs help, a hug, a laugh or anything else you will be there to offer it.

It teaches responsibility. They have a job to do and if they don't do it, it will not get done. I am trying a new system where on top of regular every day chores (like making their bed and clearing and setting the table) they each have one chore that is theirs and only theirs. They can do this chore when they want, and how they want as long as it is done by Sunday afternoon. I still need to remind (read: nag) them a bit and help some of them a lot, but I hope that they are seeing how their work matters. Our family is counting on them and they are making a real impact.

I also want my kids to know how to do these things. I want them to know how to clean their house, how to cook, how to take care of themselves. If my kids were leaving school not learning how to read, write or do math I would have some choice words to say to their teachers. So why is it okay that my kids grow up in my home and not learn cooking, cleaning and house maintenance?

We are starting small. Our oldest cooks dinner (with lots of back up support) once a week. They now all know how to clean a toilet, load and start a dishwasher and vacuum. Don't worry, I am not asking them to re-roof the house or sending the two-year-old out to mow the lawn.

I want my kids to value working. Having a job is a good thing. So is working hard even if you don't like cleaning the toilet (and who does, really?). If it is their job it *has* to get done. A job well-done is its own reward. Hmm, this is a bit of a long stretch as I am still working on this concept myself. At least we are learning together! Besides, I try to make chore time as fun as possible. We put on music to groove to and I try to have a fun thing to do after we are done.

These are big goals for a toilet brush to take on, but someone has to do it.

Monique LeBlanc

Saskatoon, Saskatchewan
thelasttimechange.blogspot.ca

Monique LeBlanc and her amazing husband live in Saskatchewan with their five children, always remembering their little one in heaven. She loves to make bread, knit, play her fiddle and, in many other ways, pretend that she lives in *Little House on The Prairie*.

Augustine was born at home on a snowy December 23, 2014.

Bonnie Way

Love is the most beautiful sentiment the Lord
has put into the soul of men and women.
— *St. Gianna Molla*

MY JOURNEY INTO MOTHERHOOD

I knew from the time I was a little girl that I wanted to be a mom when I grew up. I remember for a while considering a career as a doctor or nurse, but even before my teen years I had given up those dreams because I didn't want to spend four or more years getting an education to do something I would give up as soon as I had kids.

Yet even as I took every opportunity to hold babies at church and earn spare money as a babysitter, I sensed that this dream of becoming a mom was somehow not cool in today's society. I was supposed to have bigger, grander dreams as a woman. And so I began to bury those dreams, not to give them up, but not speaking of them.

As I finished high school, I decided I would be a writer and enrolled in a Bachelor of Arts Degree in English. This decision had two roots. The first was my love of writing; in my teens, I wrote a series of young adult fantasy novels, attended my first writer's conference and subscribed to multiple writers' magazines. The second reason was that I knew this career could fit with my dream of being a mom.

Throughout university, then, my answer to the question "What are you going to do?" was, "Write." It often got noncommittal responses like, "Ah," but that answer was more socially acceptable than my other answer. Especially since motherhood depended upon meeting a guy who shared my dreams.

In the spring of my second year of university, I went camping in Jasper with six of my girlfriends. We'd known each other since first year classes and spent a weekend celebrating the end of exams while we hiked and shopped around town. One night, sitting around the fire at our campsite, one of the girls asked each of us what we wanted to be doing five and ten years down the road. There, in that group of girls I trusted, I confided that my dream was really to get married and have kids. Lots of kids.

A couple years later, blurting out that information again cost me a job interview. I was done university, trying to find a paying job with a B.A. in English (since writing wasn't yet very lucrative), and applied for an administrative position with my alma matter. When they asked me what I saw myself doing a year from now, my mind went blank. Then I said the only thing that popped into my head: my boyfriend and I had just gotten engaged and hoped to start a family. A half-second of silence ensued before the interviewers resumed their questions, but I knew I had just blown my chances at that job.

When my husband and I got married, I felt like I could begin talking about my dreams of becoming a mom. However, when we mentioned that we wanted a large family, we were usually answered with doubt. Frequently, we heard, "Oh, just wait until you have your first child. Then you'll change your mind." Once again, I stopped talking about wanting to be a mom and have lots of kids.

A couple years later, my husband and I were living

in a new town as he started a job as a teacher. I was finally doing my dream job as a stay-at-home mom to our six-month-old daughter, and pursuing my writing while she napped. Every new person we met, however, seemed to ask the question, "What do you do?" I found myself answering, "I'm just a mom." I hated it even as I said it, wondering why I belittled doing something that I saw as much more than a job.

Being a mom was a calling — a vocation — and I loved it. Yet most of the other couples whom my husband worked with lived on two incomes. They were either childless or had their children in full-time care. My daily work of doing laundry, taking Sunshine to the park, getting groceries, cooking supper and cleaning house seemed somehow less in comparison to their jobs as teachers and lawyers and accountants.

One year later, however, my husband's job ended and we found ourselves in a new town again. We both began job hunting, searching for any way to support our family. Every time I sent out my resumé, I sensed the gap on the paper between the end of my last job as an editor and my attempts now to find a job. As resumé after resumé went out unanswered, my sense that nobody wanted to hire a mom was confirmed.

Then Starbucks responded to my resumé with an interview request. I had said nothing about my family on my application, made no attempt to explain that gap in my work history. At the interview, I lied outright when they asked about my plans for the next two years. I didn't say anything about my two-year-old daughter or the baby I was expecting in eight months. Instead, I mentioned we'd moved to be closer to our families and that I'd always wanted to work at Starbucks. When they asked if I could picture myself in management, I said, "Yes," while I pictured the maternity leave benefits six months of full-time work would allow me to apply for.

Two days after the morning sickness started, leaving me lying on the couch fighting exhaustion and nausea while Sunshine played beside me, Starbucks called to say I had the job. Could I start in three days? Somehow I got myself off the couch, went shopping at Reitman's for appropriate work attire and ordered a prescription for Diclectin from my doctor.

That was the beginning of the darkest six months of our marriage. I liked Starbucks. I discovered my skills as a mom translated easily into the coffee shop; multi-tasking came in handy when making five drinks at a time, cleaning was essential to food safety and store operation and I always got the store to-do list done by the end of my shift.

At the end of the day, however, I still came home to the housework, grocery shopping, and laundry. My husband and I were trying to juggle taking care of Sunshine, and when we both had to work, we left her with my mother-in-law. I missed bedtimes with her because I worked the afternoon/evening shift (which helped me deal with morning sickness). We didn't have friends in town, because our changing work schedules prevented meeting other people. And we knew we'd be moving on soon, so what was the point of making community only to leave it again, as we'd already done once.

In April, I resigned from Starbucks. In May, our second daughter was born. In August, we moved to a new province to return to school. My husband convinced me to continue pursuing my dream of writing by taking a Bachelor of Arts

Degree in Writing. Now, instead of saying, "I'm a mom," I could say, "I'm a student."

For a time, we attended the students' Mass at the local church. It was close to our home and we liked the priest, but after six months I told my husband we needed to find a new church. We were the only students who were married and had kids. We needed to find other families to hang out with. And so we found another parish, which had several other young families attending and hosted a weekly moms' group.

There, in that moms' group, I truly discovered my vocation as a mom. We spent an hour and a half once a week pouring out the ups and downs of being moms. We talked about breastfeeding and potty training, sex and cooking, pregnancy problems and tantrums. There, I could say, "I'm a mom," with pride. I could talk about wanting more kids without getting laughed at.

When I finished my second degree, I spent the summer thinking about the previous four years and the milestones that had led me to where I was. Juggling motherhood and student life — even though I'd only taken two or three courses each semester — had been extremely stressful. It had been hard on my marriage and on my relationship with my daughters (now three). In fact, in my final year, I had done the one thing I'd said I would never do: I put my oldest in kindergarten and my middle daughter in daycare, because I couldn't keep being both mom and student full-time.

Now that was all behind me and I had the chance to do what I had wanted to do since I was very little. I discovered I didn't have to keep trying to be more; being a mom was enough.

As I gave myself permission to just be a mom, all the little daily tasks of motherhood became a joy instead of a chore.

Now, my daughters are starting to talk about what they want to be when they grow up. They've suggested things like nun and marine biologist and "artist who draws dinosaurs." But most of the time, they say they want to be a mom just like me. And I say, "That's good." I want them to know they can be anything they want to be — even a mom.

Because I'm a mom. And I love it.

BABY'S FIRST SHOES

I bend down to pick up the pair of tiny pink shoes, and cuddle them in my hands as I carry them to my bedroom. I set them on the dresser, nudging them together. I'll put them away tomorrow, because she's sleeping now, curled up in her crib after a long day of wearing these shoes.

The shoes look tiny there – both fit in my palm. Yet already their soft leather is moulded to her six-month-old feet, the soles a bit worn from her first steps, taken while swaying back and forth at the waist, proudly grinning and clinging to Mommy's hands. On the leather, I see marks of spit-up that somehow gets on everything, though I wipe it up while she laughs at me.

The toes are shiny from the many times she's sucked on them, despite my attempts to tell her those shoes have stood on dirty floors, strange chairs, restaurant tables, park sand, green grass, car trunks and who-can-remember what else. They enchant her, these changes to her feet, and so into her mouth they go, while she smiles at me from her bent-double position, blissfully unaware that such flexibility is rare.

These shoes, her very first pair, came from her grand-mother on the occasion of her baptism. They were big then, a toe's length beyond her big toe, and stiff with being new. First attempts to put them on her feet were difficult, as she curled her toes and wiggled her feet and wondered what Mommy was doing.

Now they slide onto her feet easily, as the leather has softened and she has gotten used to the process of putting on socks and shoes.

The day that she first wore these shoes was one of the milestones that I actually remembered to record. It seemed a bit strange to be putting shoes on feet that weren't yet walking. If we carried her everywhere, why did she need them? Was I wanting her to grow up too fast by having her wear shoes? Yet if nothing else, they kept her feet warm, and soon she began standing up, testing out her legs and feet, discovering how her muscles worked, and those shoes began their job.

She'll grow out of these shoes soon, into the next pair and the next. Part of me wants to hold onto these shoes, these moments. I've been warned to enjoy this time when she doesn't need the shoes because she isn't walking yet, to hang onto the moments where she still requires me for mobility and stays where I put her down, kicking her shod feet against the grass, the couch, the rug, the bed or bending double to see if they taste any differently today than they did yesterday. But I know I cannot hold back time; all I can do is walk with her along the way, and buy her new shoes as she needs them.

BABY'S SMILES

Two teeth poke
Into a wide grin
Between rosy cheeks.
Arms wave
Conducting a symphony
Of compliments and coos.
Toes touch nose —
Button nose, like mommy's.
Teeth test toys
And fingers and food.
She's a sweetie
All declare
Always so good.
Enjoy these months
These smiles
When everything is new
For both of you.
Live and laugh
Learn and love.
Much too fast
This time will pass.

NIGHT WAKING

Into the deep drowse of dream
Comes a cry.
Fling off the covers.
Fling off the slumber.
Run — Where? What ? Why?
Moon lights the way to a baby
Standing awake and alone.

It's 3 am. Go to sleep.
Here's blanket, soother, lullaby.
My eyes are slits, yours are wide.
According to *The Baby Book*, you
Should be sleeping through the night.

Hushabye, I'll hold you tight,
Trust like a blanket wrapping us both.

Bonnie Way

Vancouver, British Columbia

thekoalamom.com

Bonnie Way has a B.A. in English (2006) and in Writing (2014). She and her husband have been married since May 2007 and have three daughters. She blogs about motherhood, books and more at **thekoalamom.com** When she's not blogging, she can be found baking, swimming or playing board games with her family.

Monique Les

Always be a first rate version of yourself,
instead of a second rate version of somebody else.
— *Judy Garland*

THE HARD—OF—HEARING MOMMY

I'm not your typical mother. I also happen to have a hearing loss, and affectionately call myself a hard-of-hearing person (HOH). I began to worry about the following:

♥ What if we can't hear her cries at night? What if our 'modified' baby monitor system we've set up doesn't work? (This was a *huge* concern for us…)

♥ How am I going to figure out what she needs when she cries? What if I can't tell the difference between a hungry cry and a dirty diaper cry?

♥ Will my daughter think I'm an embarrassment when she's older?

♥ What if my daughter wants to have a conversation with me, and I can't understand her?

♥ Will my daughter ever resent us (as her daddy also has a hearing loss) for having a hearing loss, because we'll need help from her at some point?

If you've ever heard of the following saying, you'll look at me and think — "That's easy to say, but harder to actually practice!" However hard it is, it's very true: Worry is a total waste of time. It doesn't change anything. All it does is steal your joy and keep you very busy doing nothing.

With a little babe to look after, I realized very quickly that worrying didn't do a thing for me.

Being proactive did. We found solutions to most of the worries that I listed above. Step one was to investigate any available technology that would be able to help us hear our daughter at night.

Typical baby monitors wouldn't be able to do the job for us — because, well, we can't hear at nighttime. I'm not about to wear my Cochlear Implant all night, otherwise I'd wake up each morning with a pounding headache...and moms know how important it is to have a good night's sleep! We found a Wi-Fi camera that would enable our bed shaker (I affectionately call this my vibrator) to go off via a smartphone app (snaps for apps!). Bam! We got our baby monitor system through unconventional means for about the same cost of a standard monitor.

Slowly, but surely my fears began to alleviate. Taking this motherhood thing day by day was my best strategy. I paid attention to my daughter's cries, and eventually figured out what she was asking for through trial and error. When travelling, we learned from others that our "travel" baby monitor set up (long story short, it's a less sophisticated system than the one we have at home) didn't work — and poor baby girl screamed for a while (and by a while, they never did tell us how long the screams ensued). Upon learning this, immediate guilt set in — a pretty normal reaction I would say for a new mother! Fortunately, my husband is a tech geek and he was able to tweak the system so that we wouldn't miss another 'cry out'.

Now, ten months later, I'm just starting to get comfortable with the whole concept of being a mom. Having a hearing loss can play some mean tricks on your psyche — I had many doubts about my abilities to be a good mother. I realize now that the moments where I didn't hear my daughter doesn't affect my love for her (and vice versa). I realize now that the moments where I questioned if I was doing something right is unimportant after all. I was just doing what I could do to survive. I realize now that worry is not conducive to positive action. If something fails, try something different — in my case, I had a few failures (thankfully!) and was able to solve them through logic. Lastly, I realize now that I have to live in the present, to enjoy my daughter's young life. I'll cross each bridge as they come.

Benefits Of Being A Hard Of Hearing Mommy

As the proud mommy to a ten-month old baby girl, I've finally come to the realization that having a hearing loss proves to be, in some cases, a mommy superpower. In no particular order, these are some of the benefits:

♥ When baby girl screams, I can just take off my Cochlear Implant (CI) and have complete silence. A break for the brain.

♥ When changing diapers (she absolutely hates getting her diapers changed – especially the poopy ones), I don't have to hear her ear-piercing screams. I can tell that it's pretty *loud* by how red her face gets.

♥ If someone gives me unsolicited advice on how to raise my baby, I can pretend I didn't hear it — or *not hear it* at all. Ignorance is bliss.

♥ When baby girl's toys — specifically the ones that make annoying sounds are going off, I can always turn down the volume. *My* volume. So peaceful.

♥ I am less concerned with how well I sound when I sing to her. I have a valid excuse as I'm quite literally tone-deaf.

♥ When breastfeeding at night, my brain stays half asleep (uh, hello – I'm not going to wear my CI all night long!). I've often fallen asleep with her on my boob in the chair.

♥ We recently did the cry-it-out sleep training method. As hard it was, it was mitigated by my inability to hear the full torturous experience (my heart still broke though!).

♥ While pumping milk, I'll often surf the internet in silence. Definitely a good way to avoid that mechanical pump hum.

♥ I am more attuned to her visual cues than most would be. This especially comes in handy when she needs to go to the toilet (and thereby save money on diapers).

♥ While baby girl naps, I sometimes go for one too. This means I'll take off my CI, and actually fall into a lovely, deep sleep (only to be awoken by my vibrator.) No white noise to keep me up (i.e. the radio, the laundry machine).

♥ I actually can say that I use a vibrator as part of my baby monitor system. Makes for hilarious conversations.

♥ Technology is our friend. Because of our hearing loss, we found a cheaper way to monitor baby girl rather than going for standard baby monitors. Thank you, Foscam camera and smart-phone apps.

♥ Tantrums during mealtimes are a new thing now. I'll just turn off my CI; eat my meal in quiet, while giving her the look that screams I'm not giving in. After all, that's how my mom did it with me when I couldn't hear as a kid.

♥ We know that in the future, when we need to have 'adult' talk we don't necessarily have to leave the room. Lip-reading is available to us at all times.

Ah. The awesomeness of having a hearing loss—there are moments when I feel like I can breathe in Kairos time thanks to being able to block out sound for even just a short while (ancient Greeks had two names for time: Chronos and Kairos, Kairos being 'moments of complete and utter awe' in the midst of everyday Chronos time.)

DON'T 'NEVER MIND' ME

Whenever I have a conversation with anyone, I usually miss out a few key words or sometimes sentences because my brain doesn't pick up sound the way most people experience it. A conversation will go like this:

Friend: "Oh, what a beautiful day!" (In my head, it sounds like a garbled message...)

Me: (with a blank stare on my face) "What's that?"

Friend: "Never mind."

Never mind. Ouch. That hurts.

The two single most hurtful words to a hard of hearing person. I have heard these two words over and over, and it still pierces my heart each time. Much like how every time we sin, we pierce the heart of Christ.

As a mom, I am determined to never let my daughter say "never mind" to me. When Rachel's older, I'll do my best to get her to look at me when she's talking (even if that means turning off the TV), I'll teach her that mommy needs to lip-read in order to understand what she's saying, and I'll do my best to convey to her the importance of facial expressions (without them, sometimes messages are lost in translation for me). Right now as an infant, she is reliant on facial expressions to tell me when she's happy, angry or plain content. It's relatively easy — so far. I know that when she starts talking, I'm going to be sent into a mental vortex of:

"What did she say?"

"I think she said... no, I don't know what she said!"

"Huh!?!" (scratching my head)

Fortunately, we have a great support group and they're over lots. Odds are, I'll be asking them every once in a while to help me interpret my daughter's words until I get the hang of it. As part of my concerns communicating with my daughter, I spoke to a fellow hard-of-hearing daddy friend. I asked him how his two young children communicate with him. He told me that it's not easy at first, getting them to sit (or stand) still so that he could understand what they needed, wanted or were telling him about their day. In the long run, it proved to be fabulous training for his two children — today, they are excellent communicators, and have language skills above par for their age groups. *Phew!* Good to know that it'll be a bit of a challenge at first, but once Rachel gets the hang of it, it'll be a relief.

That being said, I am looking forward to:

♥ Hearing the first time Rachel says my name (with it being French, she might call me Monica first)

♥ Realizing that I can have a mother-daughter heart to heart without difficulty (a long ways away, but this one brings a smile to my face!)

♥ Hearing the many *I love you's*

So, this is how I envision a future conversation, when Rachel's about fifteen years old.

Rachel: "Mom, can I go out with some friends?"

Me: "Sorry, I didn't catch that. Can you say that again?"

Rachel: *Hopefully not exasperated and she'll be looking at me, speaking a little bit slower and clearer, and possibly rephrasing,* "Mommmm, can I go out with some friends?"

Me: "Sure you can, just tell me who's going, where you'll be and be back by dinnertime."

A simple conversation, with some slight adjustments, would bring me such joy! It might require some patience, but then again, patience is a virtue.

THANK YOU FOR KEEPING ME

Mama loves Rachel,
Rachel loves Mama,
I love Rachel,
Rachel loves me,
Mama and Rachel forever and always!

When my little girl Rachel arrived, this was the first and only song to calm her down through her fussy moments. As bad as my voice probably sounded, it was mama's voice. There's nothing like hearing your mama's voice — even as a grown up. There are moments when I step back, look at the big picture and realize that my mama did the same things that I'm doing now for my daughter. It certainly puts everything into clearer focus.

This moment of realization made me shed a tear.

I am a child of a 'suggested' termination.

My mama got super sick when she was pregnant with me, and doctors feared I would be born with a hole in my heart, physical deformities and other unknown conditions. All but one doctor suggested termination, no doubt a heartbreaking diagnosis for parents who had been trying for eight years.

Fortunately, they decided to buck against the odds and keep

me. A precious little miracle, my father always says even to this day. Months rolled by. Their anxiety getting greater as my mother got rounder. Their uncertainty for the future completely clouded. Their lives were in constant limbo.

Then I arrived.

Tears of joy probably trickled down their cheeks (as I can imagine). However, I was whisked away to an isolation room, essentially a broom closet in those days, for fear that I'd be contagious — which I was not. One by one, tests were run, each of them passed with flying colours, except for the hearing test.

Fast forward twenty-eight years later. My little girl arrived.

Tears of joy trickled down my cheeks as I gazed upon my sweet cheeked, chubby ten pound girl after being in labour for thirty-six hours, which culminated in an emergency C-section. Like me, my daughter was whisked away to be examined — I felt a little lost for a few minutes, not knowing what was going on. It's kind of funny when you think, in hindsight, that history does repeat itself. Shortly after Rachel's examination, I held her for the first time. All the pain from labour, surgery and mental anguish was gone in an instant.

There are no proper words to explain the feeling of euphoria when you meet your little one. Each morning, when she sees my face, her face automatically lights up. I am immediately transported to that very moment when I first carried her in my arms! Having a child has been such an unimaginable blessing; before having her I had no idea how much joy she would bring me. Amidst the moments of exhaustion, I look at her and think: *Wow, I have been entrusted by God with the responsibility of taking care of this little soul.*

So, thank you mama for keeping me. Without my mama, I wouldn't be here. Without me, my baby girl wouldn't be here. There would be less joy in this world.

Monique Les

Victoria, British Columbia

thehardofhearingmommy.blogspot.ca

Monique lives in beautiful Victoria, British Columbia with her daughter and husband of four years. She is an avid traveler — swimming with the sharks in the Galapagos, embarking on a five day Safari in Kruger National Park and scaling the heights of Machu Picchu. Monique holds a Masters in Criminology from Simon Fraser University, and is currently looking for employment after taking time off to enjoy her family. Her Catholic faith keeps her grounded, and she was named after St. Monica, the first church her parents attended after finding out they were expecting. Monique was born with a profound, bilateral, sensorineural hearing loss, and has never let that stop her from reaching her dreams. In 2002, she received a Cochlear Implant and 'heard' the sound of water and music for the first time!

Melanie Jean Juneau

Katie (age 8): "Lucy, who's your favourite —
Mum or Dad?"
Lucy (age 3): "Both!"
Melanie: "Smart answer, Lucy."
Lucy: "But she's not my real mum. Mary is. God
the Father in my heart. Baby Jesus in my heart.
Holy Spirit in my heart. Mother Mary in my
heart…but I still like Mum and Dad the best!"

BECOMING A MOTHER IN SPITE OF MYSELF

I am a conundrum because I am a joyful mother of nine children. This fact seems to confound most people who expect me to appear haggard and be filled with regret or unfulfilled dreams. When people look at me, their eyebrows shoot up, their mouths drop open and they sputter,

"*You* had nine children?"

This is because I am 5' 1" and weigh 104 pounds. I was pregnant or nursing for eighteen years without a break. Even though I've lived through ten pregnancies, I am healthy, remain quite articulate and have a quirky sense of humour. This challenges the typical image of a woman of a large family as a grim battle-axe, efficiently marshalling her young charges with little time to coddle the poor, deprived dears. Surprisingly, my kids turned out well-rounded and successful, while I, who grew up with only one sister, discovered freedom and joy precisely as a mother of a large family.

I admit, by all outward appearances, I'm an old-fashioned sort of woman, a stay-at-home mother who raised her children on a small family farm. Embracing such an outdated lifestyle has meant struggling with confusion, guilt and a perceived sense of public disapproval. It took years, but I have finally reached the point where I can confidently announce, "Mothering is my call, my vocation and my witness to the world."

Forty years ago, I shocked my family and friends when I converted to Catholicism at the age of nineteen. My intelligent, liberal-thinking grandfather lamented, "My God, how did she get herself into that mess?"

Four years later, I considered continuing my studies as a graduate student in English literature. Other than that, I didn't foresee any changes to my life, which flowed smoothly. After a childhood centered around ballet lessons and books, I now enjoyed gardening, painting and growing in my faith.

Everyone thought I would become a writer, a nun, or a librarian. Then I met my husband, Michael. As Michael loves to remind me, he saved me from such dire fates. Before meeting him, I had never thought of marriage or having children. I was the least likely candidate to raise a lot of them on a farm.

When I became pregnant before our first wedding anniversary, I began to panic because I knew I was completely unprepared. I had never even held a newborn. So I got ready in the only way I knew how; I read every book I could find on pregnancy, birth and baby care.

All this studying did little to equip me to mother a fragile, completely dependent newborn. I remember how nervous I was when I held my baby in a small bathtub for his first bath. It seems hilarious now, but I admit I actually had a book propped open with one elbow, awkwardly holding it at the right page, while my baby lay in a bathtub on the table.

My husband, who was the second oldest of ten children and completely relaxed with babies, walked through the kitchen, shook his head in disbelief and said quite wisely,

"Melanie, there are some things you just can't get out of books."

Despite my feelings of inadequacy, something happened to me just after giving birth to my first child. In the delivery room, the moment I held my newborn, I forgot my exhaustion and pain. A surge of motherly love rose up in my heart, combined with awe at the miracle of creation as I examined tiny, perfectly formed fingers and toes.

There was something about my baby's trusting gaze that literally drew love from me. From my baby's first year of life, he did not have a sense of himself apart from me. His whole identity was intricately entwined with mine. On a good day, that translated into an almost magical relationship of love, the strength of which astounded me. On a bad day, it meant little sleep, for I was unable to put my son down for more than a quick dash to use the toilet or to drag a toothbrush across my teeth.

Somehow, this initial culture shock became my daily life. To my surprise, each successive baby set me free to become more fully who I was called to be: a joyful mother of nine children.

WHO NEEDS A TEDDY BEAR WHEN YOU'VE GOT A TEDDY BABY?

Even when all the kids were little, I shared the magic of babies with them. It was one of the best decisions I ever made. The other kids were so thrilled to hold each newborn that I was forced to watch the clock to make sure everyone would get a chance. It seems to me that because even the toddlers were given the privilege of holding the baby, the children bonded to one another.

Bedtime became something to look forward to for the first three months after the birth of each newest addition. I would wrap the newborn tightly in a warm blanket and let each child cuddle up to a living and breathing *teddy baby*. This quiet time allowed nurturing love to flow between both children. I think it eliminated jealousy. The focus was no longer just on the baby but on an older child *and* the baby.

As I nursed, it was easy to give the older children my attention by listening, talking, reading books, helping with homework and even playing with play dough with one hand. I can honestly say that no one resented the time each newborn demanded because we all took part in caring for the baby. Little ones ran for diapers, and older kids would choose rocking or pushing a colicky baby in the buggy over washing dishes any day.

Once I managed to relate to five people at once! I am pretty proud of that statistic. I was lying on our bed, nursing a newborn and back-to-back with my husband as he read. A toddler lay curled around my head, playing with my hair. I was fixing a knitting mistake for a seven-year-old over the head of the nursing baby and talking to a ten-year-old. This feat became a family joke.

HONOURING THE COURAGE OF NEWBORNS

An advantage of having many children is being blessed with numerous grandchildren. What I found startling about my new granddaughter, Lila, was a look of utter surprise as she surveyed the world. In the hospital, when Lila turned at the sound of my voice and looked at me for the first time, her eyes suddenly widened in recognition. It was if she thought, "Ah, so this is what you look like."

She remembered the sound of my voice from her time in the womb and, at six hours old, finally put a face to that voice. Lila had been thrust out from the safety of the womb into a huge world with bright lights and loud, abrasive sounds. Yet, it was as if she were wise, an old soul who connected with my spirit when we looked at each other. It would have been an unnerving experience if it were not so profoundly sweet.

The words of Teilhard de Chardin reverberated within me: "We are not human beings having a spiritual experience; we are spiritual beings having a physical experience."

Although Lila was helpless and fragile, she was a person with a definite personality. The looks we exchanged were not fleeting but penetrating because our eyes are the windows of our souls. Without words, we recognized each other as sisters, fellow travellers who have come from God. Lila's soul knew I saw past her appearance to her true self, just as she saw past my appearance to my inner spirit.

DISCOVERING THE FOUNTAIN OF YOUTH

Advertisers have tapped into a universal craving to stop the relentless ravages of time in the human body by pushing countless gimmicks. These products may sometimes keep us healthy. However, the secret fountain of youth is not a thing to buy but an attitude, an inner way of living in Christ.

Youth is not found in a bottle of vitamins or in a jar of face cream. Youth is found when we connect with the Source of all life deep within, in the ground of our being. There are countless ways to connect with the Holy Spirit, but, as a mother, I discovered ways to connect to this energizing Love through my children.

Children live in the present moment, fascinated by sand spilling through their fingers or an ant walking down a path. They taught me how to live in the Holy Spirit, who is also present *only* in the Now. For the eternal God, time doesn't exist.

When I concentrated on nurturing my offspring, but didn't allow my little ones to nurture *me*, I became tired, empty and resentful. If I remembered to stop for a moment, my infant touched my heart as I relaxed and allowed *my baby's* love to flow into me!

In the early, hectic years I focused on trying to carve out quiet time to sit and replenish myself. One day while nursing one of my babies, I experienced a powerful surge of love pouring into my heart from my baby to me. I started smiling, heaviness and exhaustion lifted, and joy started to bubble up from deep within me! In fact, I discovered how to let my infant's love, in union with the Love of God, restore me and flood my heart with the real fountain of youth.

SURVIVAL TIPS FOR MOTHERS

After living for more than thirty years with people who are under eighteen years old, I would pass on a few simple but effective tips to new mothers:

1. Ignore the bad and praise the good.

2. Don't get upset over messes; they happen every day, so just let disasters roll off.

3. Laugh—a lot—because a sense of humour and humility is crucial to sanity.

4. Don't worry when kids say they're bored; they soon will pick up a book or a pencil.

Now, if I could offer only one piece of advice to young mothers, I would begin by asking them, "Want to know how to avoid a temper tantrum?" There is a common image stuck in our brains of a screaming toddler throwing a tantrum on the floor of a grocery store. Even the best parent becomes a helpless victim in these situations because nobody is as miserable and disagreeable as a hungry and irritable baby or small child. This so-called temper tantrum is really a baby breakdown. Babies lack the tools to vent their frustration and anger.

Think what it's like to be in a position of total submission to another person's control, unable to meet your own needs. When I ignored the warning signs of my kids reaching their limit of endurance, I created either a clinging, whiny wimp or a screaming monster. By then, nothing I did or said seemed to help the situation. Putting our kids' needs first is never self-sacrificing but rather a form of self-preservation.

BABY WHISPERERS

Most adults are not natural baby whisperers. They simply cannot read a baby's nonverbal body language. Children, especially babies, are vulnerable and at the mercy of the large, often clueless adults, who care for them. Put yourself in a baby's situation. It must be frustrating to be tired only to have a bottle thrust into your mouth, or to have an upset mother try to nurse you when your stomach is full of gas.

This disconnect does not end once children can communicate. Nope, our adult reasoning does not always compute in an immature brain. Why, I have been told that human beings do not get their adult brain until they are twenty-five years old. Apparently, the frontal lobe that makes sane, rational decisions is not fully developed until then. This means for almost a quarter of a century, humans need a special kind of love and nurturing that will connect with them. Parents must guide their children gently, without controlling or stunting their spiritual growth.

The best mothers are willing to learn from books, experience and others, including their offspring. Good mothers need a wonderful sense of humour to laugh at their kids' blunders as well as their own. Openness to trying new tactics helps, as does creativity, but mothers need to be intuitive, listening to their little ones' body language and tone of voice. To get the inside scoop on what each child needs at one particular moment, effective mothers listen to God because He knows more about our children than we ever can.

ARE WE ALL HERE? ANYONE MISSING?

"Oh good, you're done barn chores. Perfect timing; dinner is almost ready."

"Two more minutes, everybody!"

"Daniel, I'll help with that after we eat, okay?"

"Mary, please run up and open Claire's door and shut off the music."

"Dinner is *ready!*"

"Lucy, I know you love that book, sweetheart, but remember, no reading at the dinner table."

"Where's Matthew?"

"Honey, would you lift up David into the high chair?"

"Are we all here? Anyone missing?"

Ah, dinner time in a large family.

Dinner was the highlight of the day with everyone clambering to share their news or simply squeeze in comments or opinions into the cacophony of voices. It was a humourous symphony that sounded perfectly in tune and in harmony to my ears with high baby voices, loud, boisterous little boy voices, the quavering of a male voice changing, Dad's reassuring bass tones and my calls for every one to listen to the toddler's newest word. The highlight of this often unruly symphony was the spontaneous laughter that punctuated the entire meal.

Life around the dinner table was relaxed and happy because I allowed my children to behave in age-appropriate ways. I did not demand adult perfection. The consequences of this decision were messy but well worth the time it took to mop up after mealtime. It meant not shovelling in neat, tidy mouthfuls of food into a toddler because we let little people feed themselves as soon as they reached for the spoon. It meant including three-year-olds in meal preparation, sending five- and six-year-olds running out to the garden for vegetables and letting go of pride by encouraging a ten-year-old make the dessert. In other words, we valued participation over a neat and tidy kitchen and orderly mealtime.

Now, I am reaping the rewards of decisions that sent my mother-in-law into a sputtering spiral of incredulity as she eyed my kitchen and the faces of my little people after a meal. Yet even she looks now at my grown-up kids with admiration because they all love to cook and entertain, especially for each other. Just drop by for a quick 'hello' and inevitably they will cajole you to stay for a meal. It is a simple fact that there is no better way to foster the development of a warm, supportive family than with delicious, home-cooked food and relaxed conversation around the dinner table.

WHAT IS REALLY IMPORTANT IN LIFE?

Since preschool, adults pushed us to excel, to rise above our peers. We were groomed for success, that is, to get into the best universities and snatch the most prized careers. Well, it is nice to have confidence, to fulfill dreams and to have a sense of satisfaction in chosen fields of work, but that will not make us happy.

Just take a look at the generations that have gone before us. The midlife crisis is a testament to the failure of a life focused on career advancement to the exclusion of family. Men and women bemoan the fact that they did not take time for nurturing and loving their spouse or children. All too often family life crumbled to ashes, sacrificed on the altar of success.

I want to yell as loudly as I can, "Raising children is definitely not a default chore for women who were not successful in the world of business, power, and wealth." How we raise our children will directly influence the kind of society they, in turn, create.

Do we want to live in a world focused only on the ruthless accumulation of wealth? Will we consciously create a race of humans who are cynical about family and love?

Family is crucial; it is the foundation of society. Now I see my adult children beginning their young families, and it touches my heart to know they value family as much as I do.

Just after his daughter's birth, my son turned to his dad and said, "Dad, this is the best thing that I have ever done in my life."

And, a year later, as his little daughter lay sleeping on his chest, my son said, "Now I know why you and Mum had so many kids."

RECIPE FOR CREATING A STRONG, FLEXIBLE MOTHER

Baking Pan: Faith in God, not self.

Bottom Crust: Layer 5 pounds of sheer determination (guts) alternately with 5 pounds of sinew and true grit. Make sure the crust is firm yet still flexible, so that it does not crack under pressure but bends when needed.

Spices: Sprinkle crust and each layer with pounds of laughter, which is essential to survival.

First Layer: Add liberal amounts of creativity and intuition combined with circular thinking. DO NOT MEASURE. Do not substitute with logic or linear thinking.

Second Layer: Delight in children, a shake for each kid.

Top Layer: Gratitude and thankfulness. This clear, gelatinous layer receives light and permeates every other layer.

Icing: Joy, which cannot be purchased and is pure gift.

Drink with a strong cup of black tea, steeped at least five minutes.

Melanie Jean Juneau

Rural eastern Ontario

melaniejeanjuneau.wordpress.com

Melanie Jean Juneau is a writer, wife and joyful mother of nine children and five grandchildren. Her writing is humourous and heart warming, thoughtful and thought-provoking as she focuses on revealing the truth about children, family and marriage to our modern society. Melanie is the administrator of *Association of Catholic Women Bloggers,* a weekly columnist at *Catholic Mom,* and a monthly writer for *Catholic Lane, Catholic Stand, Catholic Attachment Parenting Corner* and *Catholic 365.*

POEM, IN A MOMENT

Roberta Cottam

the clock ticks
  the fan whirs
    my pulse beats
     my mind counts
      hours of crying
       hours till morning
        hours of work
         tomorrow and today — how exhausted!
        And the thought speeds my pulse
       quick as a clock
       and she cries
           cuddles
           snuggles
           burrows
           breathes.
           Counting breaths — I can't help myself —
          always counting
           counting minutes
            awake, minutes asleep
            wishing for sleep…
             Her eyelashes interrupt
             flicker over my chin
            slow me down

            till all is still

ACKNOWLEDGEMENTS FROM THE EDITOR

I would personally like to thank my Landmark Self-Expression and Leadership Program coach, Charles Blair, who kept this project on track through many ups and downs. Thanks also to my sister Kathryn Cottam who lent an editing eye and to Laura Wrubleski for generously producing the book within a modest budget, in particular the beautiful cover art. Much appreciation to my dear friend Lieneke Norman, who listened to all my dreams as to where this book might lead, and to Petra Rutz and Irene Karoutsos for drafting submissions which were not included in the final lay-out. Your commitment to me and to this project is not unnoticed.

Special thanks to Anna Eastland who lost a child and to Monique LeBlanc who birthed a child during the process of making this book. Your continued contribution during these intense times of motherhood is an inspiration.

On behalf of all of the authors, we wish to thank our families (especially husbands and children) for their enduring support. Without their understanding, we would not have the space and energy in our lives to write as freely as we do.

And to our readers, thank you for choosing to spend your time with our stories.

Blessings,
Roberta

ABOUT THE EDITOR

Roberta Cottam

Vancouver, British Columbia

robertacottam.com

Roberta recently published her first novel, *Bluebeard's Bride*, and her short fiction and poetry have been featured in *The Claremont Review, Naming the Baby, Three Short Tales of Red* and *Fabled: 17 Tales You Think You Know*. *Shakespearian Shopping Theatre*, co-written with her sister Kathryn Cottam, was short-listed for the Arts Club in Vancouver. Roberta is also a fine artist and worked as a freelance designer for clients such as Lululemon and the social enterprise Me to We, where she collaborated with Laura Wrubleski. She holds a BFA with distinction from the University of Victoria and was a faculty member of the Art Institute of Vancouver. Roberta lives in Vancouver, British Columbia with her husband, daughter and soon-to-be second child whom she plans to deliver at home.

ABOUT THE DESIGNER

Laura Wrubleski

Vancouver, British Columbia

visualaura.net | 205trueheart.com

Laura earned her Applied Visual Communications Degree in graphic design in 2003 and recently completed the Interaction Design Essentials program from Emily Carr University. She has nearly 15 years of experience crafting beautiful images, interactive experiences and compelling layouts for large corporations, small businesses and individuals. Drawing and writing since she could pick up a crayon, Laura is never far from a pencil or a computer! She is currently maintaining a personal design and inspiration blog at **205trueheart.com** and you can view her online portfolio at **visualaura.net** She is comfortably nestled in her Vancouver corner apartment with her loving partner, Neil, and their two cuddlebug kittens, Drake and Pixie.

Made in the USA
Charleston, SC
19 November 2016